The Book of Why

Layout and design: Elisabeth Ferté
Typesetting for the English edition: Emmanuelle Lallemand

Copyright © 2003, Éditions de La Martinière SA, France
Originally published in French as **Le livre des pourquoi** by Éditions de La Martinière

English translation copyright © 2005, Éditions de La Martinière SA, France

Published in 2005 by Harry N. Abrams, Incorporated, New York.
Printed and bound in France - L 98881 b
10 9 8 7 6 5 4 3 2 1

Abrams is a subsidiary of

LA MARTINIÈRE
GROUPE

The Book of Why

Martine Laffon
Hortense de Chabaneix

Illustrations by
Jacques Azam

HARRY N. ABRAMS, INC., PUBLISHERS

Table of Contents

Why don't children ever clean up after themselves?

Maybe children don't clean up after themselves because, deep down, they hope that someone will do it for them!

Not all of us share the same idea of tidiness and yet, from birth, we spend a lot of time picking up after ourselves and putting stuff away. Much like the way we organise our belongings, the brain categorises all the information it receives, sorting similar objects together: shirts with shirts and books with books.

The reason the brain categorises information this way is so we can retain it better. If we put our socks in pots and pans in the kitchen and stored everything in the refrigerator, there would probably be something seriously wrong with our brain.

And yet, out of laziness, we sometimes put our socks away with other things that don't belong. That's how disorder begins. The problem is that parents equate a messy room with a messy brain. And a messy brain means it's impossible to learn and perform well in school.

They have a point there. Organising and putting things away, even if we use a system that only makes sense to us, leads to better organisation in life and work. Oddly enough, this starts with little things, like cleaning your room.

Why do we cry?

A fierce wind
or a great fright,
a fly in your face
or feelings of sadness,
an aggressive insect
or throbbing pain:
it's all the same for
our bodies' tear factory!
This factory doesn't distinguish
between physical
or psychological pain.
So how does the whole mechanism work
and where do tears come from?

Imagine an intelligent car
whose cleaning fluid appears
at the touch of a button
and makes even the tiniest stain
on the windshield disappear.
Much like such a dream car, our eyes
are uniquely designed to prevent
any kind of foreign element
from clouding our vision.
Our body's windshield is
the transparent membrane which
covers and protects the cornea.
Tears are our very own cleaning fluid.
And our eyelids
are our windshield wipers.

This amazing tear factory
produces on average
about half a teaspoon
of tears per day,
flowing regularly into the eye
but never spilling over.
But when our eyes are irritated,
they produce tears continually
until things go back to normal.

Your eyes and nose
can't absorb everything,
and so tears roll down
your cheeks and nose.

So why hold back?
Crying is good for you.
Tears are one of the best ways of
cleansing the body and soul and
keeping your vision clear!

Why are dessert plates smaller than dinner plates?

In the old days, rich families used to change plates at least six times during the course of a meal. Nowadays, even though we change them far less often, it is considered polite to eat dessert from a different plate than the one we use for our appetiser or main course.

It is in fact preferable to keep distinct tastes separate, and not mix them up on the same plate.

But why are dessert plates small? So small that there's barely enough room to fit three scoops of chocolate ice cream?

Can you even see the dessert?

Dessert comes at the end of the meal, so we can't stuff ourselves with apple pie, fairy cakes or other delicious treats, the way we would at the beginning of a meal, when our stomachs are empty. The size of the dessert plate is in fact directly proportional to appetite.

Soup and similar dishes provide us with nourishment. But dessert is a pleasure that has nothing to do with hunger. So, if you want a big dessert plate, there's only one solution: eat your meal backwards!

12

Why does it rain?

When the weather forecaster says to expect rain, you shouldn't always take his word for it. Nobody knows for sure what the weather will be like tomorrow, let alone in two hours. So, why does it rain?

The air is in constant motion around the earth; it moves from colder to warmer places. Warm air is light and high in the sky, whereas cold air tends to be heavier, and therefore lower. Because the water from oceans, rivers and lakes is constantly evaporating, the air is full of water vapour invisible to the eye.

When air passes over cold ground, it cools and becomes heavier. This is how fog and dew are formed.

When cold air comes into contact with warm air, the warm air rises and the water vapour it holds becomes a loud. When the drops of water become too heavy for the cloud to carry, they fall, and that's when you see rain!

Why does it rain every time I decide to leave the house?

Though the explanation of this phenomenon is simple, weather patterns are unpredictable and can change in a moment's notice. Wind is capricious, and it's not always easy to know how strong a cold or warm front will be.

Even if meteorologists use more and more sophisticated computers to do their work, weather forecasting remains a very complex practice.

13

Why are there diseases?

People have long been curious about the origins of diseases.

In Western medicine, we've grouped the causes of diseases into four general categories.
The first includes diseases caused by foreign agents.
In this category, the enemy can be an insect, a virus, bacteria, fungus, pollution, or even bad food.
That's how measles, the flu, AIDS or allergies are transmitted.

The second group of diseases are caused by an internal disorder: the body's functions are thrown off balance and cells start to deteriorate and eventually self-destruct.
Diabetes and cancer are included in this group.

The last two categories include diseases caused by "accidents" that occur at conception: these are called genetic and chromosomal diseases.
Cystic fibrosis, for example, is a genetic disease caused by gene mutations.

Grrrrr!

Because chromosomes exist in pairs, chromosomal diseases occur when there is an extra, or missing, chromosome on one of the 23 pairs normally present in the body.
A person with Down's Syndrome has three chromosomes on the 21st chromosomal pair, instead of two.

Even though we have many built-in resistors to certain diseases, it's best to limit the risks of contracting them by adopting good hygiene and respecting our bodies.
After all, "an ounce of prevention is worth a pound of cure!"

Why am I afraid of the dark?

Because we can't see anything in the dark, that's why! We're not cats, after all. Our eyes need a minimum of light to focus and decipher our surroundings.

Leave the door open! Turn on the hallway light! Don't close the blinds! Everyone has a preferred method to avoid complete darkness.

It takes just one time, one brief moment, to develop a fear of the dark. For example, when a baby falls asleep in his or her mother's arms and wakes up in a crib he or she has never seen before.

Or awakening from sleep to find your head at the foot of the bed, where your feet should be. Or trying to find the bathroom in the dark.

Poor eyesight and memory aren't the only problems exacerbated at nighttime. To this list, we should add the eerie silence of the dark, which amplifies even the faintest shuffling of leaves or creaks in the floorboards. Or the fact that in a drowsy state, we aren't in full possession of our faculties and can easily lose our bearings.

Although some children freely express their fear of the dark, adults tend to hide it. Without giving away their secret, some adults overcome their fear by never closing their curtains!

15

Why must children always obey?

Don't play with matches!
Don't eat sweets!
Brush your teeth!
Go to bed!
...what a pain!

But have you ever noticed
– for example, on those nature
shows on TV – a mother lion holding
her cub by the skin of his neck
to nudge him towards
the rest of the group?
Or a mother monkey forcing
her young ones to remain still
while she removes their fleas?

That's the way it is!
Both human and animal
offspring don't know what's good
for them at birth. Their parents need to
teach them how to nourish themselves,
bathe, and integrate themselves
into their environment. Until we acquire
our own survival skills, our parents
must teach us and show us
how to live our lives.

Think of it as
the "Law of Love". Children don't
obey because adults are stronger,
but because they are loved by them.
The most crucial role a parent
can play is to give children
the strength to live independent
lives along with the tools
to fit into the society at large.

Here's a word of advice:
the quicker you master
the life lessons taught
by your parents,
the less they will seem
like obligations!

Why don't we all worship the same god?

In antiquity, the Greeks worshipped Zeus, the ruler of the gods. To Romans, Jupiter was the ruler of gods and men. They say that the Egyptians had twelve powerful gods. Today, around eighty per cent of the people in the world have a religion, but they pray to many different gods.

To some people, there is only one god, and for others, there are many gods and goddesses. To some people, this one god is holy, but for others, gods can be perceived as evil.

Why don't we all have the same god? No one knows for sure what God is really like, so everybody imagines Him or Her in their own way. For this reason, it's impossible for all of us to share the same idea of God.

Jews, Christians and Muslims believe that there is only one Creator of the world and of men. Hindus believe that Brahma, Shiva and Vishnu are the three great divinities. It's also possible to believe in the same god but worship him (or her) differently, depending on your religion.

Each religion has its own rites. They tell us how, where and when to pray, what to eat, what is forbidden, and how to dress, so we can always be in accordance with our god or gods. Choosing which god to believe in depends on our culture and the country we're from. There are few Christians in Asia, for example, and few Hindus in the West.

Why do we fall out of love?

Poets have long declared that love lasts forever, but we express love in so many different ways: friendship, affection, admiration, familial love, romantic love…

In theory, the only love that lasts a lifetime is the unconditional love a parent has for a child. When we grow up, we all go on to love someone else.

We can't help the fact that we grow up and get older. Differences between people tend to increase as time goes on. We make new friends, develop an interest in something that only yesterday seemed boring…

Basically, we are constantly changing, and our feelings change as well. Your best friend can become your worst enemy if he or she jeopardises your friendship by humiliating you. Or the two of you can drift apart if you don't share the same mindset.

It's always sad when a friendship comes to an end. But it is important to accept others just as they are. It's all about trust: trust in yourself and in others.

Traitor!

I don't love you anymore!

You betrayed me!

why does the sky make noise?

No, storms aren't triggered by Jesus playing football with his friends or an accident occurring between two clouds, though it may sound that way. The sky's ferocious noises are actually caused by specific meteorological phenomena.

When it's very hot outside or when a mass of cool, dry air meets a warm, humid air mass, huge thunderclouds form. Inside these clouds, swirls of air movement push water droplets upward. Just as temperatures fall at a higher altitude, water freezes to become ice. Because they're heavy, these bits of ice begin to fall and turn into water droplets again, which descend from the clouds as rain.

Within a cloud, water droplets and ice particles bump into each other, producing heat, light and electric flashes: this is called lightning. The intense heat produced by a lightning bolt causes the air around it to explode with a tremendous roar: this is thunder. Because the speed of light is more than a thousand times faster than the speed of sound, we see lightning flashes before hearing the roar of thunder.

Pipe down! I mean it!

It is estimated that more than forty thousand storms occur on the earth each day. Incredible but true!

why can't we all be world champions?

World champion:
what an incredible dream!
Football, cycling, chess, you name it!
What a thrill it would be to see
our name in print, appear on TV,
and sign autographs.

Though we train and
push ourselves,
working hard for years on end…
It's still not good enough!
Not everyone can be
a world champion!

We aspire to be
someone exceptional
or do something unique,
but despite our best efforts,
we still may not succeed.
Simply put, we might lack
the physical aptitude
or intellectual capacity
needed to get where we want to be.
Or maybe the goal
we set for ourselves is too high.

Bravo!

Bravo!

Bravo!

Bravo!

However, it's better to have
your feet planted firmly on the ground
than bounce from failure to failure,
and it's best to evaluate
your own capabilities
and limitations before
setting a goal.

In Greek antiquity,
the wise men advised people
to act within their limits, and not to set
their goals too high or too low.
After all, it's perfectly fine to be
the champion of your own team!

What's inside a hill?

A group of jolly goblins who dig winding tunnels and frighten moles? No, seriously, let's ask geologists – scientists who study the earth's changes – what can be found inside a hill!

It took seven hundred million years for the earth to appear as it does today. The earth's surface looks different depending on where you are. In Britain, for example, the surface is composed of mountains, plateaus, hills and plains.

Hills are actually very tall mountains that were created during the earth's formation, but whose rocks and rugged peaks eroded over millions of years by wind, water, cold and other elements. So, in a sense, they shrank.

Some hills measure less than five hundred feet and are as flat as a pancake. The surface of the earth isn't fixed; it evolves, imperceptibly, over millions of years, and new surfaces are formed.

What about those little goblins inside the hill? Nonsense. There are only rocks, rocks and more rocks, both inside and out!

Who decided that a day would be divided into 24 hours?

It's easy to read the time on a watch or alarm clock; but a long time ago, during antiquity, people lived without them. The sun was used to tell time during the day. But what did they do at night?

The astronomers of ancient Egypt created the hours of the night by observing the stars. They noted that, like the sun, the stars rose in the east and set in the west. To observe them more easily, they divided up the sky, like a big cake, into 36 portions, or sequences.

C'mon guys! It's time!

We're coming!

They also noted that one of these stars did not move – the North Star – and that other stars rotated around it. They decided to use it as a point of reference.

When observing the summer sky, the ancient Egyptian astronomers noted that only twelve portions of the sky crossed the North Star. So they assigned each of these equal portions one hour, or twelve hours for the whole night. They figured that the day would be no different and allocated a period of twelve hours for the daytime as well. A twenty-four-hour day was born.

We have discovered sundials on tombstones, dating from 3000 BC, which relied on this measure of time.

Why don't animals live as long as humans do?

Mayflies are insects whose larvae dwell at the bottom of a lake for two to three years, but live less than an hour as adults.

The world's oldest known turtle died in 1965 at the age of at least 188. We know this because Captain Cook gave the turtle to the royal family of Tonga in either 1773 or 1777.

Scientists believe that man's natural life span is 120 years. Along with turtles and elephants, humans are destined to live the longest. But why is there such a difference in life expectancy?

For every species, the aging process is "programmed" in advance: their number of cells, and their regeneration and degeneration. But this process can be disrupted by a host of foreign elements that can shorten life expectancy.

Thanks to progress in medicine and better standards of living, the life expectancy of humans increased more in the last century than in the previous five thousand years!

But this is true only for so-called "developed" countries. In areas such as southern Africa, where AIDS has infected more than ten per cent of the population, life expectancy has decreased by 16 years in the past quarter century.

Why are we unkind?

Anyone can be unkind.
Being unkind is a voluntary act,
in which one person purposefully
hurts or harms another.
We're not born unkind,
we become it.

Anger usually triggers
unkindness and cruelty.
The feeling arises unexpectedly,
and can be difficult to control.
Just like that, without thinking, words,
blows and screams can explode forth,
like a thundering volcano.
And violence begets more violence
and screams, followed quickly
by tears of sadness,
helplessness and guilt.

We can't love everyone,
just like we can't understand
and accept everything. To avoid
explosions, a pressure-cooker is equipped
with an escape valve to let off excess
steam. We humans have words.
Talking about our feelings, asking for
an explanation or even asking ourselves
"How did I get in this state?"
often helps us calm down and avoid
hurtful words and outbursts.

Wait,
hold on, I'm
the pitbull!

26

How do aeroplanes fly?

One of our oldest dreams has been to soar through the air, see the sun up close and gain a bird's-eye view of the earth beneath us. And yet it's taken us century after century to figure out that simply attaching wings to our back isn't enough to fly like a bird!

After years of observation, exploration, rising and falling, mankind has discovered that even though it's invisible, air contains elements of force and pressure without which lift-off wouldn't be possible. So how does an aeroplane fly?

When an aeroplane first accelerates, the air around the plane's wings is divided into two parts, moving at two different speeds. As the wings are slightly curved on top, when air passes over the wing, it is pushed upwards, and an area of low pressure is created. Meanwhile, the opposite action takes place underneath. Air passing under the wing thrusts downward, exerting higher pressure on the wing, which creates lift. All this helps push an aeroplane towards the sky.

Thus, an aeroplane can take off and maintain its altitude thanks to air.

Failed again!

Why do we suck our thumbs?

Sucking your thumb gives immediate satisfaction, and it's not unusual to see babies doing it in their mother's womb.

Sucking is important in babies' lives, because that's how they nourish themselves. So it's easy to see how this natural gesture can become a source of satisfaction, calmness and serenity between feeding times.

In time, sucking one's thumb becomes automatic. The majority of children give up the habit around the age of seven, the age of "reason." What a coincidence! It's also around this age that adult teeth begin to appear. At this stage, sucking one's thumb can lead to dental and palatal deformations, as well as difficulties with pronunciation.

The age of "reason" also marks the moment when a child feels ready to grow up, become more independent, and conquer the world. So the child will naturally give up a habit he formed as a baby.

But don't panic! Seven isn't an absolute age limit for sucking your thumb. It's not abnormal for you to continue the habit after this age, it just means you're not ready to stop, that's all!

Why is wind invisible?

Trade Wind, North Wind, Mistral, Diablo, Willy-Willy, Zephyr: all of the 150 winds that blow on the earth were named after their area of provenance and/or their unique characteristics.

The Ancients believed in divine interference: when storms and hurricanes occurred, it meant the gods were angry, and refreshing breezes signified the gentle breathing of a sleeping goddess. It wasn't until the 17th century that Galileo, Pascal and Torricelli discovered that wind was more than just a simple draught.

The temperature of the air depends on the intensity of the sun's rays. Wind comes from cold areas, where the air is heavier, and blows towards warmer areas, where air is lighter. The greater the pressure between the cold and warm air currents, the stronger the wind.

It's the Wind God's little brother...

So why is wind invisible? Because wind is a mixture of clear, odourless gases and microscopic specks of dust, all of which are invisible to the naked eye.

When the air is heavy with rain or sand, we can sometimes see the wind moving, but most of the time we can only feel it or hear it moaning, howling or hissing!

29

Why do I like chocolate and not spinach?

Enjoying what we eat depends on a number of related factors: smell, taste, sensation and culture. The aptly named "olfactory and taste centre" is a kind of internal computer of taste located in the brain which analyses and interprets information sent by the hundreds of millions of sensors in the nose, palate and on the tongue.

Sour and bitter are not vital, and our enjoyment thereof depends on our particular olfactory sensors and especially on the development of our taste.

Leaf vegetables like lettuce and spinach give off a bitter taste when they are cooked, which some people find unpleasant. But when they're softened by a sauce of your liking, they can be delicious! When it comes to chocolate, everything depends on the recipe. Try taking a bite of a cocoa bean and you'll see how bitter it can be!

Tastes are divided into four broad categories – sweet, salty, sour or bitter – and are linked with memory.

Taste buds respond to different tastes depending on where they're located on your tongue: the taste buds on the tip of the tongue are the most sensitive to sweet flavours. Further down, the sides of the tongue are sensitive to salt, followed by taste buds sensitive to sour tastes and all the way at the back, to bitter ones.

Why do earthquakes occur in some places and not in others?

Our good old earth is not as stable as you might think. Things shift and crack on its surface and move around inside.

Deep within the earth's crust – the rocky shell that contains the planet's soil – lies a layer of hot, liquid rock nearly 2,000 miles thick: magma. Earthquakes occur in the area between the earth's crust and these layers of magma.

The earth's crust is divided into some twenty pieces, or tectonic plates, that float on the surface of the magma and move around at a rate of 2 to 5 centimetres a year. These plates can move apart, slide closer together, or rub up against each other. The collision of the plates' movements can result in tremendous friction. When the pressure is too great to resist, the tectonic plates can tear or rapidly change position.

These sudden movements generate vibrations, called seismic waves, which rise to the earth's surface, causing the ground to shake.

The space between two tectonic plates is called a fault. Most earthquakes occur along these faults. There are maps which locate the plates and faults along the earth's surface, identifying the geographic zones that are at the greatest risk for earthquakes.

Why do stars shine in the sky?

Since the dawn of time, a lot has been said about stars. Some of our distant ancestors thought that stars were pinned to the sky, as immobile and eternal as gods. Others thought that they were little holes created for rain to pass through.

Nowadays, we know that stars – like the sun, which is only one of the 200 billion stars in our galaxy – are born, live several million years, and then die out.

Stars are gigantic balls of burning gas (their temperature can reach over 10,000 degrees Celsius). These balls of gas give off enough energy to produce light. That's why stars shine.

But a large number of warm air bubbles are constantly floating around in the atmosphere. Once they float in front of the stars, the air bubbles steal the stars' light, and so they appear less luminous in the sky.

Astronomers think that each star has two luminosities. Apparent luminosity is the one we can see on a starry night. It varies based on the location from which we view it. The other luminosity belongs to the star itself and varies depending on its size. No matter where we look at it from, it never changes.

Why is the sky blue?

Poets have long extolled the pristine beauty of a blue sky on a warm summer day; but did you know that we actually see the sky through a 300-mile thick gaseous layer? This is the earth's atmosphere.

The earth's atmosphere is a thin layer of gas that makes up the air we breathe. Think of it as a giant scarf that wraps around the planet, protecting it from the sun's rays. This gaseous layer is what makes the sky blue. In fact, amongst the seven colours found in solar light, the atmosphere's gas molecules only absorb one colour, blue, which gets scattered around the sky.

When the sky turns red during a sunset, it means we're farther away from the sun. The sun's light must pass through a denser atmospheric layer and blue light is too far away to make the distance. Only the colour red filters through the atmosphere.

But don't let the atmosphere prevent you from enjoying the sky's view. No matter what it is composed of, the sky is always beautiful.

Can someone steal my soul while I sleep?

Only in science fiction films can baddies enter the subconciousness of goodies while they sleep. In reality, the brain remains active, and would never let anyone creep inside it without waking us first. But what is the brain doing during this time?

First, it tells the nervous system to be on the lookout. This marks the period of light sleep. Next, it tells an army of different cells to restore the body: muscles, skin, bones, etc. Above all, it lets the body grow because it is at this particular moment, and this moment only, that the growth hormone is secreted. This is the period of slow, deep sleep.

Finally, the brain refreshes itself, regroups and tries to resolve outstanding problems: this is when dreaming occurs, marking the phase of REM (Rapid Eye Movement) sleep.

Taken together, these various phases of sleep total nearly two hours, and, depending on our needs, are repeated three, four, or even five times a night! You shouldn't be afraid of sleep because dreams and nightmares aren't the handiwork of anybody but ourselves.

Forget about robbers or strangers; the images that flash before us while we sleep are merely feelings, emotions and events of the day that reappear in new ways that often help us to better understand them.

35

Why do I get carsick?

My receptors aren't doing too well...

"Hurry, stop the car! I'm carsick!" Maybe you know this phrase too well...

If riding in a car makes you nauseous, it's usually because you're not the one driving it. In a moving car, your brain processes information it didn't ask for. It's almost as though you're functioning without the brain's permission, as the brain should be giving the orders.

We all have tiny internal receptors in our ears. They tell the brain when to reposition the head. Vibrations, turns and accelerations on the road trigger these receptors, and the brain experiences difficulty registering this new information.

Next, our eyes can't focus properly because our head is moving around every which way due to the speed at which the car is moving. So the brain receives confusing information.

Finally, the pressure sensors embedded in the soles of our feet help us process the ground beneath us and maintain our balance and stability. But in a car, our feet either aren't touching the ground, or if they are, the ground is in constant motion... So it's impossible for our brains to correctly analyse our surroundings.

In other words, when we're in a moving car, the receptors and sensors in our ears, eyes and feet send unsolicited information to the brain which it has trouble processing. Carsickness is the direct result.

Why do flowers smell good?

There's no way for a planted
flower to go off in search
of a husband to make baby flowers!
Even if a flower is equipped
with both male and female
reproductive organs,
it still can't fertilise itself.

Pollen must be transported
to another flower of the same
species for fertilisation to
occur. Flowers must rely on what
nature has placed at their disposal:
wind and insects.

The most timid flowers,
those which usually
go unnoticed, rely on the wind
to scatter their pollen.
These are considered anemophilous.

Pshhhh

Others,
which are referred to
as entomophilous, are real flirts!
They lure insects with their bright
colours and enticing perfume.
Insects approach them and
easily adhere to the flower
because pollen is sticky.
Like the gluttons they are,
insects move from flower to flower,
collecting pollen, transporting it to
other flowers, thereby achieving
cross-pollination.

A flower's perfume
doesn't attract
only insects, however…
for thousands of years,
humans have tried to reproduce
these intoxicating scents to win
favours from their gods
and neighbours!

37

what is infinity?

Infinity,
what a funny word…
it stretches out endlessly,
like a long snake,
and nobody can stop it.

Infinity
is a difficult concept
to comprehend, because everything
around us has boundaries:
our house has two floors,
the garden extends from the tall
oak tree to the neighbour's fence,
and walking home from school
takes five minutes.

But it's more complicated
for things that happen up in the sky. What
lies beyond the billions of galaxies?
Where does space – that great expanse
of the universe beyond earth – end?
Does it even stop somewhere?

For centuries,
scientists have constructed
powerful telescopes,
perfecting them over the years
in order to see farther and farther away.
Space is so big that it's impossible
to know exactly how far it goes,
or if there even is an end.
The word infinity is used to connote
something that has no limits.

Maybe one day
we'll figure out where space
begins and ends, and
discover that it isn't infinite.
But for now, the answer keeps
its (endless) distance!

Why do our teeth fall out when we're little?

Dolphins are born with all their teeth, but because they have so many (some species have up to 250 teeth) it's doesn't matter if they fall out. Snakes and crocodiles can lose and replace teeth up to twenty-five times in the course of their lifetime!

As for humans, we have different kinds of teeth assigned to specific functions. Our teeth grow in two successive stages: baby teeth and adult teeth.

These two stages of teeth are formed in the interior of the gums after the embryo's second month of life. Their roots grow until the first teeth appear, about six months after birth. At this age, a child's digestive system is ready to absorb solid food.

Peek-a-boo!

But the jaw doesn't reach its full size until fifteen years of age. Before then, all those teeth would never fit in such a small mouth!

After the first four molars appear, the tooth fairy soon makes her first visit. Baby teeth fall out to make room for adult teeth. All of our teeth are fully grown by the time we turn fifteen, except for wisdom teeth, which either grow much later, or never at all.

Why are witches always wicked in children's stories?

With their hooked noses, clawed fingers, hairy chins and tousled hair, storybook witches put curses on people, eat children and transform princes into toads.

Witches do their job well: they scare us in stories so that we fear them less in real life.

Reading scary stories helps us blow off steam and rid ourselves of bad thoughts. Witches represent our bad side.

For example, we may secretly hope to unload the burden of a little sister or a mother who complains and punishes us. Isn't it better for the witch to cook your little sister in her bubbling brew? Better she does it, and not you, right?

Witches are wicked because it's always the nice guy who wins in the end. The reader of a book always imagines himself as the super hero or heroine who does good deeds, as opposed to the cruel actions of a wicked witch. In a way, the witch makes us want to be a better person.

Then again, if the roles were reversed, and the witch were the friendly heroine of the story, we would probably have no problem identifying with her!

41

Why are some people afraid of walking under a ladder?

Maybe we avoid walking under a ladder because we're afraid of getting hit by a can of paint or some kind of unidentifiable object; but to some people, walking under a ladder brings bad lack.

These people fear that walking through the triangular space formed by the leaning ladder, the edge of the wall and the ground will break up the three points corresponding to the three sides of a triangle. For many cultures, the number three signifies perfection, and shouldn't be disrupted in any way. We call this way of thinking superstition.

Superstition comes from the Latin word *superstitio*, and means "standing over" something threateningly.

The following things are considered superstitions: a black cat crossing your path, having thirteen people at the same table, finding a four-leaf clover, or playing the lottery on Friday the 13th. Being superstitious means believing that actions, colours, animals, days, and objects can be lucky or unlucky, and can alter the normal course of events.

Careful!

It's sort of like giving everyday things magical powers… If only!

How can we go on living when someone we love dies?

We can't prevent the death of a loved one. Because we love them so much, the pain of their loss can be excruciating, and we may think there's no end to the sadness we feel. But they are the ones who cease living, not you.

Our entire history is made up of people whose lives, at one moment or another, come to an end. But they will always remain a part of our family and our lives, of who we are now and who we will someday become.

Nobody knows in advance when they will pass away. Nor does anybody really know what happens to us after we die.

Death is scary, precisely because it's the greatest unknown. But we can help one another overcome this fear by making the most out of life: meeting new people, loving each other and preparing ourselves for what's to come.

The death of one person doesn't end the life of another. On the contrary, it should renew our will to live life to the fullest and to never forget those we have lost.

Why did prehistoric people have so much hair?

Because prehistoric people lived in the nude, with neither shelter nor fire, body hair was essential to their survival. But nowadays we live in a much warmer climate, and our fur slowly began to disappear during the course of our evolution. So why is it that we still have more than a hundred million hairs on our bodies?

With the exception of our eyelashes, eyebrows, and the hair on our head, our body hair at birth is extremely fine. It becomes thicker and darker during puberty. The rate of its growth and how long it remains varies in function of age, gender and where it grows on our body.

Each hair follicle is connected to a specialised gland called a sebaceous gland. This little duct secretes an oily substance – sebum – which softens and waterproofs the skin, prevents bacteria from penetrating the surface, and helps to maintain a stable body temperature. What a system!

When you're scared, angry, cold, or emotional, a little muscle on the hair contracts, causing goose bumps!

Several million years ago, when we were still covered in hair, our body hair even helped to deter our enemies! And guess what else? The stiff spikes on the spine of a hedgehog are also hairs!

Why do parents work all the time?

If you need something, call us...

... gotta go

...to work!

They leave the house at eight in the morning and often don't get home until after seven, five days a week... wouldn't it be nicer if our parents were always on holidays?

What good does it do to work around the clock if parents never see their kids? That is no way to live, no matter how much they love their job!

But sometimes there's no way around it. Work means a salary, and a salary means money to buy the things we need to eat, take care of ourselves, live, have fun, get around, raise kids, and send them to school so that they too can get a good job and work for a living... This is the way our economy works.

For our distant ancestors, more than thirty thousand years ago, two days of hunting or gathering per week was enough to feed the entire household. Today, we could never depend on hunting and gathering for our livelihood!

But being a slave to your job and coming home every night weighed down by files and papers isn't the solution. Striking a balance between time devoted to work and time spent as a family will give you the peace of mind to enjoy pastimes such as chasing butterflies and gathering flowers... with the whole family.

How do we know what we want to be when we grow up?

In the old days, we didn't question what kind of job we would have. We just followed family tradition. If you were the son of a farmer, you would become a farmer as well. And in the wealthier families, the oldest son took over the fields, the second-born son went off to war and the youngest joined the church.

As for girls, they would be married off to sons of other families from the same social class without asking their opinion. Only in rare instances could you escape the destiny that awaited you.

Today, everything has changed. There are so many fields of study and various jobs available that the choices are overwhelming.

The lucky ones have already chosen a career path. They are so passionate about a certain profession that they're prepared to move mountains to get there. Others make a career decision during the course of their studies, or later in life. But for the most part, finding a job is a matter of destiny.

What do you want to be when you grow up?

A fireman?

A policeman?

Are you kidding?

That is so last century!

Curiosity is hardly a flaw when it comes to your future. The more questions you ask about the kind of work people around you do, the more ideas you will have.

There is no miracle solution for figuring out what kind of career to pursue, but one thing is certain: the better your exam results are, the greater your choices will be.

why do we resemble monkeys?

Monkey or not?
Do we simply need
to make faces to look like monkeys?
This is a question which scientists
have been asking for over 150 years,
since the first human fossils
– dating from several
million years ago –
were discovered.
Do chimpanzees and humans
have a common origin,
a shared ancestral line?

There are undoubtedly
some surprising similarities
between monkeys and humans:
larger monkeys stand upright,
use their hands, know how
to make tools and adapt
to new environments,
just like us.

On the other hand, humans are
rather incompetent in comparison;
because we lack training,
it's hard for us to swing
from branch to branch!

Hoo! Hoo! Hoo!

The visible, external differences
between us include the shape of
our face, body hair, the way in which
we stand upright and also
our behaviour with other members
of our species. Monkeys communicate
amongst themselves using signs
and grunts of varying intensity.
Humans speak using
articulated language.

But there is an even
greater difference: humans are
conscious of being conscious.
When they act, they know what they're
doing and why. Humans can think,
reflect, remember and anticipate
what will happen to them! So if humans
are merely monkeys who have evolved
after years and years –
that's some evolution!

Why is there life on earth?

When the earth was formed approximately 4.5 thousand million years ago, it was nothing but a great big ball of red molten rock. Millions of years elapsed before it cooled down and a cloudy exterior was created: the atmosphere.

The atmosphere is a protective covering that prevents the earth from burning during the day due to the intense heat of the sun, or from freezing at night. The atmosphere is also where all kinds of meteorological phenomena take place. In fact, a billion years after the earth was formed, rain fell continuously, creating the first oceans.

Thanks to this water and the provision of oxygen, microscopic bacteria slowly began to appear and evolved into numerous living species. The earth is the only planet in our solar system whose surface is seventy per cent water.

Astronomers have observed traces of dried-up water sources on Mars, or sheets of ice on Uranus, but they've never seen a quantity of water sufficient enough to sustain life.

But who knows? Perhaps some day, far away in the universe, we may find new neighbours!

Why are some people rich and others poor?

Anyone can see that there are rich countries and poor countries, and within those countries, rich people and poor people. But has this inequality existed since the dawn of humanity?

Some people think it all started the day a man placed a fence around his little plot of land and declared: "This is mine!" After that, the urge to constantly acquire more and more led to an inequality of resources.

There's no more room!

The most fundamental human rights that each person is entitled to – food, lodging, work, health care and education – are far from guaranteed. There are still many people who are starving, homeless, unemployed, lack access to medicine or are unable to attend school.

History has shown that countries have destroyed others to reap benefits, with no regard for the plight of the people living there. Usually it's because they want to gain new territories or exploit natural resources that don't belong to them.

There are many root causes of poverty, but no one should simply accept that the poor stay poor and the rich become richer. Each country should strive for a better, more equitable distribution of wealth amongst its inhabitants. Wealthier countries have an obligation to encourage the development of poorer countries. That's what solidarity is all about!

Why do grandparents have grey hair?

Just like our skin colour, our hair colour depends on the amount of brown pigment – melanin – produced by cells to protect us from the sun's harmful rays.

The more melanin these cells contain, the darker our hair is. The range of hair colour is extensive, going from black to pale yellow, with everything in between.

When we get older, for example around the age of 40 or so, our cells become lazier, and melanin production decreases. Hair slowly begins to lose its colour, turning grey first, and then white.

Some people's hair turns grey prematurely, while they're still quite young; in most cases this is due to stress or a serious emotional breakdown which shocks their system. But often it's simply because their production of melanin slowed down or stopped too soon.

We're not going to let ourselves go grey!

Did God really create humans?

People have long wondered about their origins. Who or what gave them life? Their parents! And their parents before them? Their parents! And so on…

But if we could go back in time to the first human being, the question would always be the same: where did this first human come from?

Some people used to think that if we learned how the different species appeared on earth we would finally be able to solve the riddle of human provenance.

Nowadays, we know that there never was one first human, but many first human beings, and that they came from the same species – the primates – following a long evolution of living organisms: fish, amphibians, reptiles, and then birds and mammals.

How did we pass from one species to another? That's precisely what scientists would like to know. But their theories, experiments and observations will never answer the question of whether or not God created human beings.

Many different cultures and religions tell their own stories about how God created humanity. But they're not in competition with scientists, nor do they speak on their behalf.

Actually, these two groups are not even asking the same question. Scientists want to know how humans came to be. The writers of religious texts want to know why life exists, and why humanity in particular exists. The authors of the Bible, for example, thought that everything that exists was created by God.

At what age do we fall in love?

Anyone who can answer this question is extremely clever, because there is no minimum age at which we fall in love. Loving someone or something is part of what it means to be human, and it begins at birth.

But how can we distinguish love from friendship or admiration for another person? It's a question of time, reflection and experience.

Those who yearn to become one with another person, like babies in their mother's womb, confuse love with infatuation. These people forget that love, like friendship, is built on respect, trust and freedom. Even if love at first sight exists, true love must be built over time.

It's unlikely that someone can go through life without heartbreak. But keep in mind that these heartbreaks are a learning process that pushes you forward to the next stage of adulthood.

And whatever happens, know that love in all its forms is what gives us meaning in life, at any age.

Wait until you're in nursery school!

But age doesn't matter!

Why does fire burn?

Our distant ancestor *Homo erectus* is credited with the discovery of fire, at least 500,000 years ago! More precisely, he learned how to start and control it, because fire has always existed. But what is fire exactly?

Fire is a combination of light, heat and flames, triggered by a substance that burns. This can be wood, charcoal or gasoline but also a blanket, book, or our hand!

Fire is like a big monster who is prepared to devour anything in its path. We can run our finger quickly through the flame of a match without feeling anything, but there's no way we can leave it there for a second longer without burning ourselves. Our skin is resistant to heat, but only up to a certain point.

Every year, hundreds of thousands of people burn themselves with various degrees of severity. The causes are often due to sources of intense heat which people are not careful about: heated milk which boils over, a forgotten clothes iron, or staying out too long in the sun. Regardless of the degree of heat, getting burned is serious, and it's advisable to act quickly.

Even if learning to control fire has contributed greatly to our evolution as a species, there's still no excuse to act like "Vulcan" or other fire gods; fire can be very dangerous!

Why are planets round?

Why aren't stars actually
star-shaped or planets
shaped like cubes or pointy hats?

Because in space,
everything revolves around gravity,
the force of attraction
that pulls bodies towards each other.

The shape of a sphere
allows all parties to be as close
as possible to each other.
In a cube, the corners would be at
a disadvantage, because they would be
farther away from the centre.

So, bodies which approach
each other spontaneously
take on a rounded shape.
It's a little like how people naturally
form a circle around someone
in order to see him or her better.

why do we die?

Everything in nature deteriorates, grows old and disappears. All living things eventually die. Scientists have tried to convince us that we can delay the aging of cells and repair them, but there's no avoiding the fact that one day we will die. So what's the point of dying?

Obviously, if everyone were still living after seven million years, we wouldn't have that much room left on earth. But we can't justify death merely because we don't have enough space to accommodate everyone.

Oh, I'm dying!

Whining doesn't help...

Although we may never know why we die, we can at least try to come to terms with it.

Many cultures and religions believe that death does not mean the end of life. They think that even though a person physically deteriorates after death, his soul lives on, or is reincarnated, which means that his body comes back as another person and lives a whole new life. This is what Hindus believe.

For people in Africa, the dead allow those still living to communicate with the world beyond.

In other religions, death is merely a stage on the path towards God and divinity.

Why aren't we all the same?

Dark skin, light skin, green, blue or brown eyes: nobody really looks like anybody else, not even twins. This is what genetics, or the science of genes, is about: determining what makes each of us unique.

Genes carry our hereditary information inside our bodies' cells. The information contained in an individual's genes is like a little book in which our genetic code is written, exclusively for us. This is what we call a genetic card.

Even if what we eat, where we live and the climate can affect our physical appearance – people who live in cold climates don't look like those who live in tropical ones – there still aren't specific Asian, African, or European genes.

All humans share the same genes, but some appear more frequently than others, depending on a person's race or ethnicity.

How lucky we are to be built the same way and yet still be so different from each other! Only objects can truly be identical to each other.

Why are tomatoes red?

Because they're fully ripe, that's why! Ok, but why are they specifically red? It's actually not that simple…

The colour of an object depends on three things: the nature of the object, the light that shines on it, and how your eyes see it.

Here's a little experiment: if you shine white light on a tomato, for example the sun, which contains seven principal colours – red, orange, yellow, green, blue, indigo and purple – what happens? The tomato, like a sponge soaking up water, absorbs all the colours except red. Only the red is reflected back to the white light. So you see the tomato as red!

How would I know?

Now, try shining a green light on the same tomato. What happens? The tomato seems to turn black! Why? Because the green light doesn't contain any red, the tomato doesn't reflect any colour. The absence of colour makes it black.

Why do children always want to act like grown-ups?

Adults don't like it when children try to imitate them. But though they may not realise it, grown-ups also imitate their elders: their parents, their heroes, either real or imaginary, famous people, religious figures, or athletes.

But why would someone want to imitate someone else? Today, psychologists tell us that children need role-models to help them shape their own identity.

They learn a number of important things from adults: right from wrong, what's acceptable or dangerous, and so much more.

When they get older, children continue to follow the examples that have been set for them: they can either adapt them to their own way of thinking, or reject them entirely and invent new ones.

But in the meantime, children will continue to think that grown-ups' lives are full of adventure. Whatever they're doing is always more exciting!

61

Why don't we all have the same skin colour?

Experts see us all as having the same colour skin. In some ways, they're not wrong. Seen through a microscope, all skin, regardless of colour, contains cells filled with the same brown substance: melanin. Melanin is a pigment which protects us from the harmful rays of the sun. Melanin production increases in response to greater sun exposure.

Several million years ago, the first inhabitants of the earth lived in Africa, where the sun shines intensely. Their skin was very dark because it adapted to the particular climate in which they lived.

When different peoples conquered new territory in cooler continents, they no longer needed as much protection; over time, their skin lightened.

The same pigment can be found in all types of skin, but the quantity varies according to race or ethnicity.

Fair-skinned people love to get a suntan, but be careful! Nature may have given us natural protection, but melanin can't prevent us from getting sunburnt. Our best protection can only be found in tubes: suntan lotion!

Chocolate   Vanilla   Vanilla-Strawberry

Why is there night and day?

Here's an interesting experiment:
bring a ball into a dark room.
Place the ball on the ground
in front of a flashlight.
Roll the ball around and look!
Only one side of the ball
is illuminated.
The other remains
completely dark!

The same
goes for our days and nights.
Imagine that the flashlight is the sun,
an enormous spotlight
that never shuts off,
and the ball represents the earth.

The earth rotates,
from west to east,
at 1,000 miles an hour each day;
each time one side passes
in front of the sun, it's daytime,
but for the rest of the world,
it's nighttime.

Think of it this way:
it's not the sun that rises
and sets. We're the ones
who choose to turn
our back to the sun!

It's my turn!

No, mine!

Everyone gets a turn!

Why do we learn some things at school that seem useless?

It's not easy trying to work out if something is useful or not! A lesson learned at school may seem useless now, but how can you be sure it won't come in handy five years from now? What is your definition of useful knowledge, anyway? Simply learning how to read and count? Isn't there more worth learning?

In school, we acquire indispensable knowledge about the universe, human beings, and the techniques they have invented. Later, depending on what we want to do, this knowledge will help us choose a profession.

Of course, some things may seem less important than others, but they are useful in that they pique our curiosity, open our mind, and give us the tools we need to learn new things, resolve problems and adapt to new situations.

But we can't discover life's treasures on our own. We need teachers to help us understand, explain and retain this knowledge. This acquired knowledge helps us to communicate, think, invent, and live side by side in society.

In a word, this knowledge will help you look beyond the tip of your nose!

Why do doors close?

A little window...
a door, open to the sun…
In the villages of yesteryear, houses didn't have many openings, not only due to cold weather and the threat of robbery, but also because a tax was charged to people based on the number of doors and windows they had in their homes. Doors were often made in two pieces, so that the top part could open for fresh air to circulate.

So why do doors close? Because a closed-off space is safe and intimate, giving a person the opportunity to be alone. Closing the door gives you your own little universe, and everything that belongs to you is protected inside. This way, you can shut out bad weather, robbers, strangers, or nosy people who happen to pass by!

In certain warm and humid regions, such as in the Amazon, you can still find houses without doors. These houses are held up by wooden pillars and their roofs are made of woven palm leaves. In these homes, fresh air is always welcome. But if you're looking for privacy, the hammock is the place to be!

Which door?

Why aren't children's stories true?

What do you mean? Pumpkins that transform into carriages, magic wands and Prince Charming – all of this isn't real? They're only stories to help children fall asleep?

That's right! Even if we cried with the heroine, cheered on the hero, sailed off on a boat full of pirates or liberated planet Z44, the characters from these stories aren't real; they merely sprang from the imagination of the people who wrote them.

An imaginary story will never come true. It's called fiction. The stories aren't real because the characters in them don't exist in everyday life, like you do. However, although stories aren't real, they can still more or less resemble real life.

Imagine if, starting tomorrow, all the heroes, monsters and princesses from our stories actually came to life! What would there be left to dream about? What could we invent in our minds?

I'm quite aware that you're not real!

After all, would we really want to cross paths with a real, honest-to-goodness goblin, running wild in the streets?

67

Why do parents always find out when we've done something bad?

Do your parents have a "third eye", a kind of hidden camera that captures your every move when they're not there? No! Then how come they always end up knowing everything? They pay attention, that's all!

Face it: it's not that hard to figure out that you used nail polish when there are traces of it all over the carpet! Nor is it a big mystery that you played in the hay when it's practically spilling out of your shoes!

And even if you greet them innocently and obediently, they can't help but think that you're hiding something... The more you squirm, blush or mumble when answering their questions, or look anxious, the more certain they will be that you've done something bad!

What chocolate?

There's no need for a "third eye" or a hidden camera, because parents are extremely observant! But even though they can usually guess what you're up to, they can't know everything!

And in several years, when you confess certain childhood memories, rest assured that they're in for a big surprise!

What's the point of prayer?

A prayer
is a kind of speech
addressed to someone
who lives in an entirely different
world from the one in which we live.
We can pray to God,
divine beings, or to supernatural
powers as a way
of communicating with them.

Each religion
has its own rites
with particular gestures, clothing,
and sacred places of worship:
temples, churches,
pagodas, forests,
synagogues, and mosques.
There are also specified
times for prayer. It's not the prayer
itself which is powerful,
only the person to whom
it is addressed.

Whether
we pray alone or in a group,
prayer has a clear objective.
Much like a call,
it asks for a response.
And one always hopes
that a prayer will be answered.

...Hello God?...
...I'm listening...
...Hello?...

The connection is bad today.

There are
many different
reasons why we pray.
For example, one might
pray for good fortune,
or to prevent misfortune,
to pass an exam,
recover from an illness,
earn money, or protect
oneself from enemies.

However, in most cases,
prayer is simply a dialogue
with a higher power.

Why don't we all speak the same language?

Speech specialists differentiate between speech and language. Speech refers to all our means of expression – the sounds, gestures and signs that enable humans to communicate with each other. Language is a combination of specific words that belong to a community.

English, Chinese, Berber, Inuit: we don't all speak the same language because we all belong to different communities. However, the sounds and structure of similar words prove that some distinct languages share the same root.

Languages evolved through contact with others. French, English, Spanish, Sanskrit, and many others are called Indo-European languages. There are over one hundred different families of languages in the world.

English, French, Chinese

Though speech is innate, language is learned. People have always dreamed of speaking the same language, and some have even invented languages, using words that everyone can understand, without success. English is the most widely spoken language in the world today.

We use language in order to speak; it allows us to express what we want to say. Nobody can speak on your behalf and everyone has the right to speech, no matter what language you use to express yourself.

why do we put people in prison?

If everything were permitted, there would be no need for justice. Everybody would do as they pleased with little regard for the welfare of others. The strong would soon squash the weak. That's why when someone deliberately commits a crime against someone else – robbery, rape, violence or even murder – that crime does not go unpunished.

One way of punishing a criminal is to deprive him of his freedom. If society decides, after judging his case, that someone is a threat to the life, security and welfare of others, that person is put in prison for a certain amount of time, depending on the crime committed. By putting criminals behind bars, society can both protect itself and punish those who have disobeyed the law.

Depriving a citizen of his rights as well as the freedom to move about and communicate with the outside world is considered by the courts a proper punitive measure for the harm inflicted on that person's victims. If the crime is so severe that no compensation is possible, the criminal will be locked up forever. Well, at least for the rest of his life.

Why are spiders so scary?

Peeking out from their hiding places and lurking about with their eight hairy legs….Eeeeeeek! You tremble just thinking about them creeping up on you, opening their venomous fangs and biting you while you sleep!

It's true, spiders don't have a great reputation. But maybe you need to get to know them a little better, without bias, before they can win you over!

Spiders may be carnivores, but they don't suck your blood like mosquitoes do, which are, fortunately for us, eaten by spiders. Spiders only feed on insects.

There's no denying that spiders have venomous glands and fangs which they use to bite and immobilise their prey. But there's no need to exaggerate! Given a spider's size, the quantity of venom they possess is negligible. With the exception of some of the most dangerous species of spiders – which you're unlikely to encounter, since they live in faraway places – their bite isn't fatal.

Need more reassurance? Are you wondering why spiders still bite us at night, when we're asleep and not bothering them in the least? Blame it on a chance encounter. The spider isn't on a mission to bite you, but when it spots your leg, how can it resist?

Why do people say the dead go to heaven after we bury them?

People have always thought that the sky was where the gods lived high above our heads, keeping company with the mighty sun, lightning, and the stars.

Some people compare heaven to a father and the earth to a mother. Our ancestors feared that heaven would fall on their heads, and they also feared the underground, which they thought was full of evil people who held the dead hostage.

Hey, you, up there!

In the Christian faith, when we bury someone who dies, we say that his spirit leaves this world and ascends to Heaven. But it's actually just a metaphor.

In some religions, one mustn't utter God's name out of respect, so heaven is used when speaking about God.

The expression "going to heaven" is used in everyday language. But nobody actually lives in the sky after he or she is dead and buried.

Why do people feel pain?

The brain is in an ideal position for controlling pain.

Oh, boy!

I have such a bad headache today!

The sensory receptors in our skin, muscle, veins and internal organs respond quickly to extreme heat or cold, strong pressure or injury and send messages from every inch of our body to the spinal cord – the nerve centre which transmits information from the brain to the body – at the speed of about 100 feet per second. When you get sick, your red and white blood cells act on these receptors and cause pain.

But your sensitivity to pain depends more on memory, education, stress and fear than on the quantity or quality of your receptors.

It's perfectly normal to hate going to the dentist to get your teeth cleaned or getting a handful of dust in your eyes; the receptors are highly concentrated in these areas, one per millimetre in the eyes or teeth!

There's no shame in having pain and saying something about it, but it's often difficult to express the extent of our suffering. That's why doctors have created a scale ranging from one to ten; the purpose is not to rank us, of course, but to better understand our pain.

Why do we dream?

The more we sleep, the longer our dreams are: ten, twenty, even thirty minutes in length. Sometimes we remember them, sometimes not. But it's not easy to figure out why we dream.

Some people think that dreams symbolise something profound in our lives, and that they should be interpreted in order to grasp their meaning. In antiquity, for example, dreams were thought to be messages sent by gods. In Egypt, psychics were summoned to interpret the dreams of pharaohs.

In Africa, as in other traditional cultures, healers might dream of the cause of an illness, as well as its cure.

Some people believe that dreams are a bit like films: they can appear in colour or black and white, each with their own set design. They express our everyday worries, fears, and desires in a unique way.

Finally, some people dream when they're awake and don't realise it. All of you daydreaming in the classroom are included in this group!

Why do we bite our nails?

There are as many answers to this question as there are people who bite their nails. Keeping in mind that in Britain alone, an average of one schoolchild in three suffers from this habit, an entire book on the subject wouldn't be enough to explain it!

Everyone has a reason for biting their nails. But wearing gloves or painting your nails with foul-tasting nail varnish is only a temporary solution to the problem. If you want to successfully kick the habit, you have to work out why you started it in the first place.

I quit...

Imagine yourself as Sherlock Holmes, Hercule Poirot or any other famous detective and try to figure out when and where you bite your nails.

Is it at home? At school? When you're alone or with others, and with whom? Does the urge come about when you're bored or anxious?

If you keep track of these fateful moments, either mentally or by jotting them down in a little notebook, this awful habit may in fact disappear on its own. Constantly caught in the act of biting, your unconscious will slowly lose its grip on the mutilation of your fingers!

Do plants talk to each other?

No,
plants don't talk, they sing!
Haven't you ever heard them?
You can hear them whispering
softly in the hollows of ditches,
on the riverbanks, and in the summer
wind. But seriously, how would we
even know if plants talked amongst
themselves?

Some scientists
say that although plants
don't talk to each other,
they can still exchange
information by way of
chemical gas emissions.

For example: "Be careful!
Predators are near."
Plants that are being aggressively
grazed upon by animals send this
gaseous signal to neighbouring plants.
Having heeded the warnings, these plant
can then defend themselves by giving of
a indigestible substance. This helps
discourage animals with even
the most voracious appetites!

But if the grazers
feed normally, plants don't need
to send their defensive signal,
because they don't feel
threatened.

Sometimes
we forget that plants are living
organisms…plants can easily live
without us, but we can't live
without them! That's as good
a reason as any for respecting them!

Why do cats and dogs hate each other?

Isn't this just a myth taken from cartoons? An animosity created by humans between pets who in fact have no reason to be at odds with each other?

Although they're both hunters, cats and dogs have very distinct hunting techniques. One can spend hours waiting for a mouse or bird to come within paw's length, while the other will keep his nose close to the ground, following the scent of his prey until he closes in on it.

In nature, fellow predators don't attack each other; rather, they ignore one another. They keep their hunting ground, and their prey, to themselves.

In farms and households, pets are well-fed by their owners; they hunt as a pastime, or to impress their owners. It's no wonder that a dog would be tempted to chase after a cat if he sees one dart across his path. It's all in the name of fun.

But for the most part, if nobody bothers them, dogs and cats actually get along quite well.

What good does it do to believe in God?

Before
thinking about the reasons
for believing in God – its usefulness
and the strength of our faith – we should
ask ourselves what we mean
when we say we believe in God.

We can just
as easily believe
in Father Christmas,
ghosts or extraterrestrials.
Why? For the sake of comfort,
thrills and daydreams.

Believing in God
doesn't mean
that you should
blindly accept everything
written about God. On the contrary,
being a believer means
that you use your intelligence
and good judgment to seek the truth.

More than anything else,
believing in God means wondering
whether a god exists beyond
the world that surrounds us,
and whether what we say
about him (or her or them) is true.

Ohhhh!

Father Christmas

Does the pursuit of
this truth have some kind of purpose?
For some theologians (theology is
the study of religion), believing in God
means believing in life, and the energy
that allows us to grow. For others,
believing in God also means
believing in mankind, because it
represents God's true self.
For all of us, belief in a god or gods
demands that we act
in accordance with our faith.

Why are wars fought?

Violence between two groups occurs when one group steals something that the other group possesses.

In prehistoric times, our ancestors fought each other in order to seize new, fertile lands in which to settle.

Nowadays, wars are fought because of boundary disputes with neighbouring countries: these are known as territorial wars.

Some people refuse to share their land with other people whose roots, culture and religion differ from their own, so they fight in order to impose their ideas and way of life on another group.

Some groups don't rely on just their army to fight battles, but adopt new strategies, such as terrorist attacks or hostage-taking.

However, in 1945, in the aftermath of the Second World War, the countries of the world decided to work together to prevent more wars from happening in the future, and pledged to help each other both economically and culturally. These countries founded the UN, the United Nations, because "peace is the only battle worth waging."

Why are girls different from boys?

All the secrets of our genetic make-up are contained in the nucleus of our bodies' cells, in the form of microscopic rods called "chromosomes". Humans have forty-six chromosomes. Twenty-three of them come from our father and the other twenty-three from our mother.

When a sperm implants itself in the egg in the uterus during conception, the paternal and maternal chromosomes group together to form pairs. The twenty-third and last chromosomal pair determines our sex.

Hello girls!

Chromosomes going for a walk

The sex chromosome given by our mother is always X, whereas our father's can be either X or Y. They are called X and Y because these letters resemble their shape. There's a fifty per cent chance that the last pair will be either XX, a girl, or XY, a boy.

Because our cells differ depending on whether we're a girl or a boy, not only do our visible reproductive organs differ, but our bodies function in different ways as well.

So is all of this just a simple matter of letters in the alphabet? Not quite. If our bodies can influence our behaviour, then, contrary to what we've believed for centuries now, there wouldn't be any difference between girls and boys when it comes to feelings, intelligence and even physical force, only prejudice. How girls or boys grow often depends on their family and the society in which they live.

Why do we get jealous?

I hate it when my little sister gets to stay at home all day with my mum while I'm at school. I can't stand the idea of my best friend going to that other kid's house for the weekend! I feel so let down when my dog pays more attention to my dad, even though I was the one who played with the dog all day long.

Hold it! Stop everything! Jealousy can ruin your life and your relationships with others.

But the feeling is not easy to control.

Jealousy comes about when a person lacks confidence in him or herself, thinking something like: "I'm not good enough to be loved". Jealousy describes both the heartbreak of seeing someone else enjoy something we can't have and the fear of losing what we already have.

Jealousy can be overwhelming at times; it can make us believe that everything is better elsewhere.

All of us are susceptible to feeling this kind of suffering at one point or another in our lives. When we start to feel jealousy, we should make an effort to stop it in its tracks because otherwise it can really ruin up our relations with others. Worst of all, jealousy prevents us from taking care of ourselves and making the most out of what we already have.

Why are some people bald?

Each person has approximately 100,000 hairs on his head. These hairs grow at a rate of about one centimetre per month.

That means that an average of twelve centimetres of hair grows on our head each year!

The lifespan of one hair lasts anywhere between three and eight years, and it can replace itself up to fifteen times during the course of a lifetime.

When a person becomes bald, it's because their hair replacement cycle stopped too soon, and as a result, their stock of hair is depleted.

You're invited to my birthday party.

Tomorrow I'll be eight years old!

Are there many invitees?

Three, if I don't fall out before then.

Why is it we're not upside down when we're on the other side of the earth?

That's what you think! Everything depends on your point of view. Seen from high up in space, the earth looks a bit like a pin cushion. We, the people, are like pins, sticking straight out from our clay ball. Some of the pins are upside down; others are right side up or on their side.

Gravity is what plants us firmly on the earth, like the pins on a cushion, pulling us in like a magnet. Gravity is the force that makes all bodies attract, regardless of what size they are. The greater the size difference between two bodies, the stronger the attraction between the big and the small.

Can't wait for tonight!

Because the earth is round, its gravity is the same all over its surface. That's why we remain on the ground no matter where we are geographically in the world, and why the rivers descend from the mountains or a balloon flying overhead eventually falls back down to the ground.

Gravity is also the thing that ensures that the moon rotates around the earth and the earth around the sun, without either of them falling onto each other.

So unless you fall on your head, you will never find yourself upside down on the other side of the earth!

87

Why can't we stop ourselves from lying?

At around the age of two, a child may attempt a few white lies, just to make sure that his or her parents can't read his mind. Think of it as a rite of passage in the formation and affirmation of his or her personality. If you're all alone on a desert island, you can make up as many stories as you like, but these aren't considered lies. Lies require the participation of at least one other person.

A lie can either be "useful" or "compensatory". But how can you tell the difference between the two? When you know that you've done something bad and refuse to admit it out of fear of punishment or betrayal, you tell a lie that is useful to you: you omit the truth for the sake of convenience.

Candy??? ...Really?... Where?

A compensatory lie, on the other hand, is told when you invent or embellish a certain event in your life for the sake of making it more exciting in the eyes of others.

It's not always easy to tell the truth. That's why sometimes it may seem easier to lie. But no matter what kind you tell, lies always lead us on a downward spiral which may eventually prove too difficult to reverse.

Truth requires courage, but it brings instant relief! It's up to you to decide which path to take!

Can wishes come true?

Have you ever seen a shooting star?
They say it brings good luck!
Make a wish, and it'll come true.
Great, but how? To whom, exactly,
do we make the wish? Who has the power
to make our wishes come true,
with the simple wave of a magic wand?
Unless luck is always on your side,
there is actually little chance of
wishes becoming reality.

Happy New Year!
Here's to your health!
Good luck to the newlyweds!
These types of wishes are one way
of warding off bad luck. But even if
we try with all our might to make
these things come true, it's not always
possible. We can't intervene with fate,
because it doesn't depend on us.
We have no control over illness
or death.

But
there are also the kinds of
wishes that are like vows we
make to ourselves
– the vow to be truthful,
to not cheat or to practise
non-violence. In these cases,
we decide whether
or not these wishes
will come true.

Why won't our parents let us get a dog?

So who's going to take the walking fleabag out? Who's going to feed him? Who will take care of him when he gets sick? And who will comfort him when he's all alone?

If your request to get a dog provokes an avalanche of questions from your parents, your best bet is not to insist. Obviously, your parents just aren't ready to adopt your hairy friend.

Even if you swear to your parents to take full responsibility for the dog, they probably won't believe you And they're right. A dog isn't a toy that can be left in a box unattended.

No matter what breed it is, a dog has his own personality, with its qualities and faults. Dogs need their space, and take up a lot of it, too.

You should ask yourself if the circumstances are right for a dog to be happy in your home first, rather than forcing the issue and risk losing him after a mere two months.

Furthermore, you should learn as much as you can about canine behaviour. If dogs feel threatened, they defend themselves by attacking and biting. You shouldn't adopt a dog on a whim.

A dog lives an average of twelve years – a big responsibility. Loving him may not be enough. The whole family should want to adopt a dog, that way there will be fewer bitter arguments when the dog misbehaves.

Why do we have to go to bed at night?

Because sleeping upright isn't comfortable and sleeping well is necessary for living well!

Think about it: we spend a third of our lives asleep. That means that a 60-year-old has spent 20 years of his life sleeping! It's hard not to think that all that time was wasted. So what actually happens during the night without our knowledge?

All day, our brains accumulate new information, control all the movements of our body and rummage around deep into our memory bank to recall information that might come in handy. That leaves no time for sorting and cleaning.

After long hours of work, the brain is exhausted, so it sends signals to us, like itchy eyes or yawns. There's no use fighting it, you have to go to bed! The brain needs to re-establish order. And if we prevent it from doing so, revenge is around the corner: confusion and comprehension difficulties ensue!

To work well, you must sleep well...

ZZZZ

The amount of sleep a person needs varies depending on the amount of time his or her brain needs to regroup.

Children are constantly learning, so they need more sleep than adults. A baby needs more than sixteen hours of sleep a day, and about ten hours are sufficient for children aged 6 to12.

You figure it out! What time should you be going to bed?

Thematic Index